Words of
HOPE

To:

Mrs. Gregg

From:

Colin

1984

Copyright © 1976 Lion Publishing

Published by
Lion Publishing plc
Icknield Way, Tring, Herts, England
ISBN 0 85648 055 X (casebound)
ISBN 0 85648 301 X (paperback)
Albatross Books
PO Box 320, Sutherland, NSW 2232, Australia
ISBN 0 86760 200 7 (paperback)

First edition 1976, under the title *A Word of Hope*
Reprinted 1977, 1980, 1982, 1983, 1984

Photographs on pages 15, 23, 41 and 45 by Phil
Manning; all others by Lion Publishing/David
Alexander

Quotations from *Good News Bible*, copyright 1966,
1971 and 1976 American Bible Society; published
by Bible Societies/Collins

Printed in Singapore by Tien Wah Press (PTE) Ltd

Words of
HOPE

FRESH AS THE MORNING

Yet hope returns when I remember this one
thing:
The Lord's unfailing love and mercy still
continue,
Fresh as the morning, as sure as the sunrise.
The Lord is all I have, and so I put my hope
in him.
The Lord is good to everyone who trusts in
him,
So it is best for us to wait in patience—
to wait for him to save us . . .

LAMENTATIONS 3: 21-26

REJOICING IN HOPE

Now that we have been put right with God through faith, we have peace with God through our Lord Jesus Christ. He has brought us, by faith, into the grace of God in which we now stand. We rejoice, then, in the hope we have of sharing God's glory! And we also rejoice in our troubles, for we know that trouble produces endurance, endurance brings God's approval, and his approval creates hope. This hope does not disappoint us, for God has poured out his love into our hearts by means of the Holy Spirit, who is God's gift to us.

ROMANS 5: 1-5

WE SHALL SEE GOD

How I wish that someone would remember
my words
and record them in a book!
Or with a chisel carve my words in stone
and write them so that they would last
for ever.
But I know there is someone in heaven
who will come at last to my defence.
Even after my skin is eaten by disease,
while still in this body I will see God.
I will see him with my own eyes,
and he will not be a stranger.

JOB 19: 23-27

OUR GUARANTEE

If Christ has not been raised from death, then we have nothing to preach, and you have nothing to believe. More than that, we are shown to be lying against God, because we said of him that he raised Christ from death—but he did not raise him, if it is true that the dead are not raised to life. For if the dead are not raised, neither has Christ been raised. And if Christ has not been raised, then your faith is a delusion and you are still lost in your sins. It would also mean that the believers in Christ who have died are lost. If our hope in Christ is good for this life only, and no more, then we deserve more pity than anyone else in all the world.

But the truth is that Christ has been raised from death, as the guarantee that those who sleep in death will also be raised.

1 CORINTHIANS 15: 14-20

THE SOURCE OF HOPE

May God, the source of hope, fill you with all joy and peace by means of your faith in him, so that your hope will continue to grow by the power of the Holy Spirit.

ROMANS 15: 13

WHOEVER BELIEVES WILL LIVE

Jesus said:
'I am the resurrection and the life. Whoever
believes in me will live, even though he
dies; and whoever lives and believes in me
will never die.'

JOHN 11: 25-26

TRUST IN GOD

I depend on God alone;
I put my hope in him.
He alone is my protector and Saviour;
he is my defender,
and I shall never be defeated.
My salvation and honour depend on God:
he is my strong protector;
he is my shelter.
My people, trust in God at all times!
Tell him all your troubles,
because he is our refuge.

Men are like a puff of breath;
mortal men are worthless.
Put them on the scales and they weigh
nothing;
they are lighter than a mere breath.
Don't put your trust in violence;
don't hope to gain anything by robbery;
even if your riches increase,
don't depend on them.

PSALM 62: 5-10

NEW LIFE

Let us give thanks to the God and Father of
our Lord Jesus Christ! Because of his great
mercy, he gave us new life by raising Jesus
Christ from the dead. This fills us with a
living hope, and so we look forward to
possess the rich blessings that God keeps
for his people. He keeps them for you in
heaven, where they cannot decay or spoil or
fade away. They are for you, who through
faith are kept safe by God's power, as you
wait for the salvation which is ready to be
revealed at the end of time.

1 PETER 1: 3-5

GOD'S PROMISE

Show me how much you love me, Lord,
and save me according to your promise.
Then I can answer those who insult me,
because I trust in your word.
Enable me to speak the true message at all
times,
because my hope is in your judgements.
I will always obey your law,
for ever and ever!
I will live in complete freedom,
because I have tried to obey your rules.
I will announce your commands to kings,
and I will not be ashamed.
I find pleasure in obeying your
commandments;
I will meditate on your instructions.

Remember your promise to me, your
servant;
it has given me hope.
Even in my suffering I was comforted,
because your promise gave me life.

PSALM 119: 41-50

OUR GLORIOUS FREEDOM

I consider that what we suffer at this present time cannot be compared at all with the glory that is going to be revealed to us. All of creation waits with eager longing for God to reveal his sons. For creation was condemned to become worthless, not of its own will, but because God willed it to be so. Yet there was this hope: that creation itself would one day be set free from its slavery to decay, and share the glorious freedom of the children of God.

ROMANS 8: 18-21

FLOWERS IN THE DESERT

The desert will rejoice,
and flowers will bloom in the wilderness.
The desert will sing and shout for joy;
it will be as beautiful as the Lebanon
Mountains
and as fertile as the fields of Carmel and
Sharon.
Everyone will see the Lord's splendour,
see his greatness and power.
Give strength to hands that are tired
and to knees that tremble with weakness.
Tell everyone who is discouraged,
'Be strong and don't be afraid!
God is coming to your rescue,
coming to punish your enemies.'

The blind will be able to see,
and the deaf will hear.
The lame will leap and dance,
and those who cannot speak will shout
for joy . . .
Those whom the Lord has rescued . . .
will reach Jerusalem with gladness,
singing and shouting for joy.
They will be happy for ever,
for ever free from sorrow and grief.

ISAIAH 35: 1-6, 9-10

THE LIVING GOD

As a deer longs for a stream of cool water,
so I long for you, God.
I thirst for you, the living God;
when can I go and worship in your
presence?
Day and night I cry,
and tears are my only food;
all the time my enemies ask me,
'Where is your God?'

My heart breaks when I remember the past,
when I went with the crowds to the house of
God,
and led them as they walked along,
a happy crowd, singing and shouting praise
to God.
Why am I so sad?
Why am I troubled?
I will put my hope in God,
and once again I will praise him,
my Saviour and my God.

PSALM 42: 1-5

ABSOLUTELY SURE

Abraham believed and hoped, when there was no hope, and so became 'the father of many nations.' Just as the scripture says, 'Your descendants will be this many.'

He was almost one hundred years old; but his faith did not weaken when he thought of his body, which was already practically dead, or of the fact that Sarah could not have children.

His faith did not leave him, and he did not doubt God's promise; his faith filled him with power, and he gave praise to God. For he was absolutely sure that God would be able to do what he had promised.

ROMANS 4: 18-21

GOD'S CHILDREN

See how much the Father has loved us! His love is so great that we are called God's children—and so, in fact, we are. This is why the world does not know us: it has not known God. My dear friends, we are now God's children, but it is not yet clear what we shall become. But this we know: when Christ appears, we shall become like him, because we shall see him as he really is. Everyone who has this hope in Christ keeps himself pure, just as Christ is pure.

1 JOHN 3: 1-3

GOD'S CONSTANT LOVE

The Lord watches over those who fear him,
those who trust in his constant love.
He saves them from death;
he keeps them alive in times of famine.

We put our hope in the Lord;
he is our helper and protector.
We are glad because of him;
we trust in his holy name.

May your constant love be with us, Lord,
as we put our hope in you.

PSALM 33: 18-22

FULL OF COURAGE

May our Lord Jesus Christ himself, and
God our Father, who loved us and in his
grace gave us eternal courage and a good
hope, fill your hearts with courage and make
you strong to do and say all that is good.

2 THESSALONIANS 2: 16-17

'LET HOPE KEEP YOU JOYFUL'

Love must be completely sincere. Hate what is evil, hold on to what is good. Love one another warmly as brothers in Christ, and be eager to show respect for one another. Work hard, and do not be lazy. Serve the Lord with a heart full of devotion. Let your hope keep you joyful, be patient in your troubles, and pray at all times.

ROMANS 12:9-12

OUR ETERNAL LIGHT

I will bring you gold instead of bronze,
Silver and bronze instead of iron and wood,
And iron instead of stone.
Your rulers will no longer oppress you;
I will make them rule with justice and
peace.
The sounds of violence will be heard no
more;
Destruction will not shatter your country
again.
I will protect and defend you like a wall;
You will praise me because I have saved
you.
No longer will the sun be your light by day
Or the moon be your light by night;
I, the Lord, will be your eternal light;
The light of my glory will shine on you.
Your days of grief will come to an end.
I, the Lord, will be your eternal light,
More lasting than the sun and moon.

ISAIAH 60: 17-20

DO NOT BE SAD

We want you to know the truth about those who have died, so that you will not be sad, as are those who have no hope. We believe that Jesus died and rose again; so we believe that God will bring with Jesus those who have died believing in him.

For this is the Lord's teaching, we tell you: we who are alive on the day the Lord comes will not go ahead of those who have died. There will be a shout of command, the archangel's voice, the sound of God's trumpet, and the Lord himself will come down from heaven! Those who have died believing in Christ will be raised to life first; then we who are living at that time will be gathered up along with them in the clouds to meet the Lord in the air. And so we will be always with the Lord. Therefore cheer each other up with these words.

1 THESSALONIANS 4: 13-18

NO MORE TEARS

The Sovereign Lord will destroy death for
ever!
He will wipe away the tears from everyone's
eyes and take away the disgrace his people
have suffered throughout the world.
The Lord himself has spoken!

When it happens, everyone will say, 'He is
our God! We have put our trust in him, and
he has rescued us. He is the Lord!
We have put our trust in him, and now we
are happy and joyful because he has saved
us.'

ISAIAH 25: 8-9